THE
DAUGHTERLIEST
SON

A. Loudermilk

Swan Scythe Press

Swan Scythe Press

Department of English
University of California, Davis
One Shields Avenue
Davis, CA 95616
http://swanscythe.ucdavis.edu/

Editor: Sandra McPherson
Book Design: Eric Gudas
Cover Photo: *Widow,* by A. Loudermilk
Cover Design: Mark Deamer

The Daughterliest Son/A. Loudermilk
ISBN 1-0930454-10-4

Grateful acknowledgement to the following journals and books in which some of these poems appeared: *Big Muddy: Journal of the Mississippi River Valley, Cider Press Review, The Gay and Lesbian Review, The James White Review, The Madison Review, The Mississippi Review, New Voices: University and College Poetry Prizes 1989-1998* (Heather McHugh, ed.), *Porcupine, Rhino 2000,* and *Tin House.*

CONTENTS

DARING LOVE

THE RADIUM DIAL

GREAT-AUNTS & POCKETBOOK WOMEN

DARING LOVE

DARING LOVE

I am daring love to be anything else,
to be on its best behavior wicked, to be heartache
in its prime. Love, nod yes, the noggin
of a great disease. Make chain gangs by design,
love; be phantom brawling the nursery, be darkness.

Love, a cooing shadow when a stranger
takes me into his car. Love is my spiced breath,
love cuts teeth. Love unwinds iambic vines
down unrhymed alleyways, jeweled yet innocent weeds
casually blooming the balled tongues of children.
Love dedicates itself, all ruby-sucked thumbs,
to the stewing cradle at the foot of a stranger's
gut. Tell me truth, love: why want his mouth
that toils like a bad taste after the mint
of the moon?

Just leave husk and gristle. I dare you—

be the reason my mother hated to be touched.
Thirty years with a man who refused homecomings
and proms, married without mentioning love. My mother.
Every night she bleached the coaldust out of his clothes,
tasted in his mouth the coalmine, the scuttle, the coal.
You are that smoked winter, love, admit it. You waltzed
his black lung, her wallflower cancer. The ICU nurse
said my mother loved me. Love, are you an empty stare

as the heart, your celebrated domain,
latches its last door?

I am daring love to be anything else,
to be heathen in a red room, to be God's love
for Job, to be kicked dog. Grind your spotlight
on the daughterliest sons. Leave a little despair,
love, be what the least of us can claim.

INHERITANCE

My mother's duty, some polecat heirloom—
to lounge and not lounge, goldleaf bruises
upside her cheek. So lovely, so lovely

no one dared to look. My mother is dead
and all over my father's house I drape apology,
bathe face-down deep in gunpowdered roses,

rich with meat grease. Getting it, getting it
done. Strictly his son. The secret: whimperless
quiet, a flotsam stock on the stove. Mother is dead

and all over my father's house I wear her jewelry,
her words unspoken. On the last day of her life
she died. Left me. This dynasty. My inheritance:

a hamhock, the loudest noun.

AGORAPHOBIA

Little man winter in the waxpaper apron, summer needs gagging
quick while the hot plane of its face is still
turned away. Curtains pin themselves here by noon, shadows
solder these rooms. The strongest lamp-bulbs have broken

their filaments. When the macaw on its black cage
stretches its clipped wings, the sound of feathers
startles me; like the whole house

breathing out in a rush, like someone
cracked the door. Closed the door is mother.

Open the door is father.

NOT EVEN DOUBLEWIDE

Light comes on. Smoke breaks out.
They—in nightclothes, in fits—
open the blue trailer door, fall
to the dew and scream at my fire.

They think I am still asleep
inside the burning blue trailer.

There are houses with so much
banister and window and hearth.
Houses that never stopped at redlights.
Houses without the hazards on.

We had little.
Little burns quick.

MEMA'S HAT

Sometimes they vomit with heart,
the nurse on the phone clips her sentence.

Between nausea and an oxygen tank, my mother's
mother continues to smoke. Salem 100s. She always
smoked with perfect posture and lipstick. In an all white

housing project in Jonesboro, quadrupled and sewn twice up

the middle, on a bedsore that wants bone, she's got three rooms
to sail: recliner, microwave, bed. She watches westerns,
she's quit her story, she tucks her cordless phone

into the apron pocket of her walker, she's due a permanent.
Where went that strut? The heels clicking like accountants....

Now me, walking through a crowd I remember myself as a woman

walking through a crowd remembering herself as a boy
parading through the house with Mema's hat
on crooked. I've got the kind of name that tiptoes.

I've got elders to respect. I've got a stroke under my bed
reminiscing the left side of her smile. I've got other things
to do. My mother would rather be home watching the satellite.

One more time, the nurse tells us, *and her body*
won't take it. As if her body could go on strike

from her opinion. Spitfire unto backfire, her name is the kind
that chases other names around with a hoe. Her name starts
with a secret L. Her name changed seven times in three states.

The midday weather drenches the Missouri bootheel, floods

the tri-state, and she speaks of 1937 and all that water
coming right up the steps, up the steps of the post office
where the boys gathered. And my mother's father, *he'd be*

sitting there where there wasn't anywhere else to go

and I would just go wild inside. She presses her fist
to her chest. Mema that loved hard. Mema that drank

40 years, lit up half the twentieth century.

TALK LIKE A SAILOR

We never love each other with our mouths
open & only when it's flat drunk dark do we fuck
facing—when I kneel at his mouth, the confessional,
& whisper to the little red priest inside,

I've lied, I told my lover I despised him.
(Honesty: a neckline he only buys plunging,
his bitten kiss there chromatic, blooming.)
My criminal has a handsome face, dark eyes

like hours of suspicion, moments of trust. I look
prim next to my criminal, our joke on this subdivided
district so 2nd Baptist. Talk like a sailor, says he.
Cuss a blue streak. He adores my indelicacy

at night, when it grifts him to sleep. Under
his right jaw, lunar shaving scar. I know
should I endear his flaws, he'd never forgive
mine. Night idles on its axle & I play him

by the goatee, spit toothsome songs about stars
falling & petty cash, room keys & ice
buckets, zirconias & hostages & that time
we took pictures & this heart my risked

fortress, my throttled valentine. Like a sailor,
he says. *I'll give lousy eulogy*. Cuss a blue
streak. *Hatred is loving too hard*. When he wakes,
I call him a bastard, make the bed with old fire.

He is podunk. He thinks he keeps me here.
I am jugular. Jupiter's riddle. I stay.

THE UNDESCENDING MAN

The man in my mouth who sings falsetto
has nothing to do with the woman who flashes a blur
of peter & kootch behind a tolled curtain. I took a swim

with a boy diver & surfaced hermaphrodite. I don't know
how to love myself out of such waters. On stage I freak
myself down the middle: one breast injected with paraffin

for the sake of show. My girl leg shaved. Spitcurl
opposed to sideburn. I am all I need on a desert island,
the ticket grinder sells me. I'll trade a kiss & my vote

for a little tender catcall & your boots off. The price
to see behind the trap door in my costume is the answer
to this question: Who about me do you hate the most?

In the shadows of a single hermaphrodite, who might you love?

GEORGETTE WAS A HIP QUEER

O let me out. Let someone come in.

Dainty grotesque, momma's misfire, screaming fairy buckshot
over Brooklyn. She's got the rag on tonight, stardust,
red spangled gstring & a marcel wave. Swinging, swinging.

The john isn't Vinnie; he's good for 20. She's gangplank
& *un bel di* in overnight falsetto, femme de crème &
ellipsis. He's good for 20, the john that isn't Vinnie.

Pushbutton knife + the circling boys + underfoot the ricochet
+ Georgette (jerking bobbin threaded with catcall) + blade
dilated under streetlight = her shoe full with blood.

There's bennie in the bouillon; she rides darkness
unto stars, she eats the roach. Somewhere between centrifuge
& flight, Georgette is the queen of birds.

Vinnie laughing (twang of blade) = handkerchief tourniquet
x cab ride on cobble, home **x** Arthur her brother, confiscator
of benzedrine **x** gstring **x** mother **x** bedrest **x** days **x** nights

with mercurochrome on the stab wound. If she were the only son
she would not be down, now. Locked down, how the bedroom
is still & bright. Every light on. There are no dark corners at home.

Let him come in. Mother forgiveness I want him. Unhinge
the doors, he is there. On verges of thresholds, Vinnie
& I in cobalt sky. Bird high. (We're swinging—

BUCKSHOT

Eunice, daughter. Prodigy. At three played
boogie. Did "Darktown Strutters'" on the sly

for her daddy. Nothing but church & anthem for her mother,
the minister, whose tongues or silences certified the day holy

or not. Did Bach
       like math
for white ladies. On the other side of eighty-eight
       keys, adding up
to compensation, her blues

played with eyes closed, hands ecstatic—the first black
classical pianist. Almost. Rent snagged her in Atlantic City; she
                                  hushed

drunks with Rachmaninoff. At the bar between sets she sits in a
                                chiffon dress
drinking milk from a tall glass. She changes

her name.

Nina Simone, a local rumble. Bethlehem's duped star.
Ezekiel's wheels carouse under the mahogany of her piano while
                                  royalties

get pinched. She does not own her own songs. Her contralto is a
                                   bruise
on the air. Black is the color of her true love's hair. Vengeance is
                                   mine

sayeth the songbird. *Life* accuses her of jungle jazz, shebang & Afro
topknot—pride rasping on its edge. She is called Priestess, scary
                                   charmer, fire

breather, ghostly
        yet barking.
Witch Doctor. Pirate Jenny. Obeah. A household name
        for revolution.
Extremist. Extremely realized.

Regal. Raunchy. Silken. Singed. Her piano on Carnegie's stage
                                   heaves
like a freighter. She plays the emergency ward. She commands the
                                   scene

or condemns the scene, fucking the house over when it goes to the
                                   bar
during a ballad, during the showtune for which the show hasn't
                                   been written

yet.

Tax evader. Rioter. If you'd been there when they called your
                                                    mother
Auntie you would have burnt the whole goddamned place down.
                                                    You damn

Mississippi, Birmingham, Atlanta. *It is finished.* You fly to Africa.
                                                    Expatriate.
Prophet: *You're all gonna die & die like flies.* Slighted Diva—her blade

switch-happy & daring.
            You Al Capone,
I'm Nina Simone. 20,000 at Randalls Island. 500 at Village Gate.
            Twice she asked them
to keep it down

while she tended her garden in the south of France. Two teenagers
scandalizing their own poolside with racket. So buckshot,
                                                    scatter-shot, over

the hedge she fires back. Princess Noire.
                        Superstar. Right now. *Right.*

Now.

NO MOON, NO CURTAIN

[*the stage out of season: black and striked.*]

You're leading me, after eleven-thirty at night, through the darkened wings of a closed theater. [*in a paranoid hush....*]

Stage-left, a disassembled night sky gathers dust. A wicker-backed wheelchair stage-center is turned on its side; you spin its wheel—*spokespokespokespoke*. The black curtains, dead-heavy, hooked and gathered so high above, where tiers of catwalks go unseen.... You want to show me. A staircase spirals up the backstage wall, and we climb into rising heat. You want to show me secret places. We will break open secret places.

At the third tier—ropes taut against the wall, and the stage a suicide away—we peer over the railing at a wide strap of aluminum tied there and hanging like corrugated Rapunzel halfway to the floor. You gently shake it by the edge, and bring storms. "Thunder," you announce. "Pretty neat, huh?" [*a stock phrase, delivered flatly.*]

The fourth level, neither catwalk nor floor, but a tight series of girders from which hang the curtains, fatal lights, and pulleys swigging rope. You spit through the girders and count seven. I spit. And count. [*a proud nine.*] I win. We are alone. Finally,

the roof, its satellites: no more no less catatonic than prehistoric birds perched in sleepy August midnight. Their stillness dominates the rooftops and I think of space, time, humidity, all things conveyed silently. Down again, such a long drop. Down again, thundering, startling the curtain. Down again, into the blank drama of an empty theater. No one is watching us. We can be cohorts, thieves, eyeing the pocketable. Spotlights irregardless, we are audienceless and anything can happen: no security, no heckling, no applause. With blind footing and night vision [*in a darkness similar to opening scene*], you take me to a roost above the orchestra pit.

We look down at a stage that has nothing to do with us, listening for distant noises, hints of the dormant score of set-building. We watch absence in full swing, its idle plot rocking. At times like these, when no one in the world could possibly interrupt, romance splits, like a cell: confession, demand. You answer: "I don't want the moon."

[*no curtain.*]

MEMA'S VENTILATOR

On the first anniversary of my mother's last period
we stand on opposite sides of her mother's deathbed

realizing she can't die on her own, her last breath
hooked, hung up, waiting, like a coat, to be put on.

In the already cold of herself she waits for machines
to let her go—let her breathe herself out of the neither

here nor there.

NURSE, *A FANTASY*

I've come to worry   under his roof again.
I've come to live   with a dying man
who doesn't know bed   from bedpan. My father,

his body is mine now.

He doesn't know me from Adam.
Like we never hated each other.

HOSPICE RATTLE

Teeth slip when I speak a word
I taste blood with prayer
There are no nurses to call for
living in the last chamber

Outside the walls a helicopter
plays the menace, plays the buzzard
Living in the last chamber
lost moths riot the floorboards

There is no counter to clockwise
living in the last chamber
where a gaining light downstairs
beckons moths breathing ether

Living in the last chamber
with only murmurs of physicality
the debilitating conversation
of sickness and its body

FUNGUS

A completely separate kingdom of living things.

When he says mushrooms, I assume hallucinogenic,
congregating like a suicide cult in some wasted dirt basement.

But no—gourmet,
a mute wilderness jarred, bedded, shipped. Not portabello either
but oyster, herd of pink

for caterers two states away, he brags, passing me the bowl,
our eyes cashed. He is nineteen junior and I am twenty-eight
untouched, still

with babytooth. We talk mycology,

of edible and poisonous,
of the smell in his clothes: *like chloride of lime,*
like an old potato cellar, like anise; alcoholic or alkaline
or shy; oil rags, rotting

fish, sweet like almonds, chestnut
blossoms. I tell him, "I read of an old man
raising mushrooms in an abandoned air-raid

shelter." With the space of half a person between us,
this sweet boy named Dealer—crop-tender in the 24hour

night, shepherding his sordid clique, his gang
in kid leather—he says, "You know they call it the fruiting body."

His legs, all lank, shift away from me. "And some are luminous
in the dark." He looks at me and I look away, knowing

he's not asking me to be brave, thinking how I shook
the last time he stayed over, my cotsprings betraying
me jittery. He whispered. I trembled

for morning. Tonight we play nintendo
until outside the unelectronic sound of birds disturbs us
and light threatens to make us overnighters

once again. *"The phenomenon of luminosity,"*
I read to him from vol. M,

"of phosphorescent light in certain species of fungus,"
at 6:30 a.m. with a backache, *"can be observed after dark
or by introducing the fruiting body to a dark room."*

THE RADIUM DIAL

THE RADIUM DIAL

How to tell hot spots in winter? The snow's
lost to mud, yokel dogs tumored. He's no liar,
the only geiger counter in town—always on duty

in Death City, Illinois. 125 counts per minute,
250 counts: the beery woods
behind the high school a hot spot, landfills
hum a sick steam,
route 6 trailers court their radioactive outskirts,

and the Dial—dismantled by the government
(brickdust by boiler into
armed portions) and buried all around town—
still in its own absence ticks

beneath the lot where it stood
40odd years at 500 counts per minute.

*

1983 on 1932:

"If you've got money, you've got it
licked, the whole world."

"This is a picture of the girls that all
worked at the Radium Dial. They all worked
with my sister. And that was the time
of the Depression. And all the girls worked
with her and they just like my sister all

painted the faces of the clock."

"Peg's trouble started when she had a tooth pulled."

*

1932:

Littler
like the clock's her hands daintied time itself
with the all-American convenience of glowing
in the dark. It took radium
and a skeptical brush to spook the clock's expression,

to give 3 a.m. the whisper of 3 a.m. without a light on.

Radium Dial girls by the hundreds were 16
and tricounty, 18 in fur collars, 19 and 20
on the town. (They didn't know of Madame Curie's isolation
of pure radium from 1 ton of pitchblende? Didn't know gardens
laced with radium grow tomatoes anti-clockwise? That radium
as an element "tends to accumulate in the bones"?) They were 21
and newlywed, 22 and late again. Dial-painters,

attending to one numeral at a time
around the clock. Sometimes 1's first; five 1's,
two 2's, then 0 and the commoners. Southpaws
might start at 5's paunch. The odds have angles, there
are hips on an 8. 9 is hunchback. 4 a doomed house. 11,
twins. 12, disciples. With every second hand iota,
every speck of afternoon, the girls twirled as trained

"for a finer point"

dwarf brushes in their mouths.
And the superstitious began with 7.

*

WWII:

In bedrooms everywhere radium hands accuse

radium minute rings of losing midnight
to that other 12.
                        A two-faced little
wall-clock aperch the theater's EXIT
tells the wrong time to abandoned credits.
                        Ouija boards
gleam yes in cellar, no in closet. When spirits
fail, so the ad goes, coax 'em
                        with radium. Even
grandfather

is radium-handed. As is

the oven timer. The barometer. The north star's
gauges ripen at dusk on our pilots' dashboards.

The most popular bombs fall branded
with radium crosses. Watches everywhere
                              watch back.

*

78s played when they x-rayed her. Mrs. Marie Rossiter
tapped a thumb knuckle on her collar bone. Biannually
strung up for atomic research, her body (classified

dial painter) set nuclear exposure standards,

got vaulted for body-burden radioactivity assessment.
"Different record?" the nurse enquired, restrapping her
busy arm. Marie's disposable slippers twitched
to the floor. "A waltz?" (Her body's secret:
contamination. Her secret body

a hot spot,

porous, to-be-broken. Irredeemable. Lest she forget
her friends died regularly. Lest she forget the priest
even he kept his distance, housecalling the eucharist

and splitting.) "Minuet?" With a jug of pee,
the bloodworks,
and a tarot of x-rays: how could Marie not know

that one day soon (like Charlotte's arm lost
at the shoulder, like Margaret's neverhealing jaw,
like all the tumors here and there, breasts amputated
then children) a car accident

would twin her legs terminally

hideous below the summer hemline
and housebound. "All through now.

Put your slippers on."

*

1952:

On tv. Nevada. Under a sofa

in their Sands Hotel room, Lucy
stashed her geiger counter.

Ricky disapproved of her uranium hunting.

Under the sofa, Lucy's geiger counter clicked
in fits over guest star Fred MacMurray's wristwatch

when he bent down to tie his shoe. Radium gag

begets car chase.

*

1945:

Radium imported for clocks reprocessed
into polonium blasts a light only a blind girl
half way around the world could fathom.

Gadget complete. Should we have the chaplain here?

*

1932:

The factory geared-up palpitated
gossipless. "You were too busy

to talk." Every room a hundred girls
making money,
turning out alarms, illuminating the ons
and offs. Marie's trio, wasting

their break, scraped
shine from the morning jars, painted each other starry

in a broom closet, one glowering,

another stippled
burlesque. Mutton-chopped. Cyclopsed. Ritzy. A mutiny
minor in a factory groped to the boiler with so much

shine...its smirk so pretty
in the dark, its blizzard's tail, its brillig foot
clawed like a tub's, its cricket noise everywhere.

GREAT-AUNTS
& POCKETBOOK WOMEN

FOR THE GREAT-AUNT WHO DIED BLONDE

This is not a true story
but names have been changed
to protect the never-so-innocent,
the high strung yet house-trained,

the big mouth. She's blonde for good.

In aluminum, blue with satin
interior, demure but shop-soiled—buttoned
up in the wool she wore to weddings, tacky
with toothpaste droppings—she looks
like hell boxed up
to go. Her nieces pair words: folding

& chair. A game from: vacations &

psychoanalysis. Jo says thunder, Maggie
answers lightning. Deer & tick. Canker
& sty. Hanker & chief. Cheap

& casket. Good. Bye. Never again
to sigh over Sinatra. Never again

will her roots show.

FOR THE GREAT-AUNT
WHO COLLECTED CLOCKS

When they all strike at once I'll be dead
she said
every time her clocks staggered the new hour

When they strike all in a row it's crib death
little breaths
purling one last three a.m. in the nursery

When all they strike is midnight midnight
palindromic
cuckoos excoriate their minute hands

When striking cabal they all stand alone
mentholated baritones
tall in dark corners & each a husband

THE GREAT-AUNT WHO COLLECTED
CLOCKS MEETS THE BURGLAR

She's forgot to turn the clocks back an hour & when
they ring they'll ring four when it's three & she gets
up at six so tonight swigs an extra breath every second,

every second she stares at midnight, digital in its scandal

with the moon skyridden. How they conspire against her tides
into sleep, into sleep, into sleep: into nightmaring the cellar
door unlocked & silverware drawers wrenched across a red kitchen

linoleum, premiering the butcher knife in a black man's hands.

She's forgot to set the clocks back an hour & when
she goes to church in the morning only she will have lived
this hour no one lives, this hour between one second & the next

disowned with every clock she winds minus for daylight

savings. Blindly, she makes port of every room keeping time.
Upstairs, the alarms: her room & the guest room where sisters
now sleep, where her eldest son wept curse words & stashed

whiskey before his father died. After. Still

there are these nights (she swears) when shots ring out
in a deuce of bells, when the burglar breaks a window
& the getaway night revs, when the ambulance never arrives

in time, when the clocks and all their arabics & romans

grieve not. Downstairs, the grandfathers: in dimestore nightlight
she opens them like robed men. Takes the hour. She hears
         breathing
& footsteps in the kitchen. She hears breathing & footsteps

in the kitchen. Catches her son taking twenty from her purse
         again.

THE POCKETBOOK WOMEN
OF YOU-BE-DAM HOLLER

1.
The pocketbook women beg nothing
exotic: neither
britches nay crewcut, reading light
nay altar. They babysit their uppermost
blousebuttons. Practice math on zipperteeth
with backbent bobbypins. Simply

dressed in uncashable checks,
a pocketbook woman
chats breathy as a peephole peddler,

greets respectfully her senior furniture,
keeps my kindergarten picture
in her blue new testament
miniature: I'm John one of three
troubled sons, 16
& suicidal. *"In Jesus' name,"*

up snaps her head from the blessing
so we quick shut our eyes just to open them,
       this spasmodic amen in the sweat
       of her kitchen. Soupspoons
       & sinkholes, wyandotte hens.

2.
Ever-racking unweeded graves
with plastic all-occasion sprays of faded
roses, pocketbook women hum over great-aunts aslew
on memorial day, uncles on april fools,
wandajune all july, & always a widow
from the easter obituaries. Pocketbook women
        bury pocketbook women, marry
        tacklebox men, raise
        boys on frog-gigging, girls
        to go krogering.

3.
Twice-seasonly permed with terminal curls,
a pocketbook woman
enters any room permanent first,

followed then by that foremost
gargoyle purse, anvil blunderbuss,
gallon-fat, perfect fit
for grocery cart babyseats, its twinbead
clasp snapped gangrene with fingerprints,

its idiot
straps attentive as rhubarb, its bull-leather
genuine with brimstone, distended with polkadot
rainbonnets & hankies hobo'd
with circus peanuts & horehound
cough drops & daddy's billfold
tendered with two dollar bucks
& a judas coinpurse
splitting the seam of its smileyface
scattering her birthyear nickels to mix
              with the spare & longlost,
              the pocketbook chaff.

A MARVEL TO MYSELF AM I

they sing. The Two-Headed Girl   with the hyphenated name:
Millie-Christine, *united African twins*, born slave first or
freak? $30,000/two-in-one.   Millie is the girl on the left

side of the party frock.   Elegance ridiculous on the auction
block is ironic at a dime museum. Double-baby once upon
a time got kidnapped   & toured; private audiences peered

over crib bars. 2 arms 2 legs   each. Hearts beating

like Radica-Doadica.   He ran with them no further
than England, where ma & master with Monimia
their mother won them   back. If you spy half the moon

one night & the other half   another night, is it siamese
when full? At the point of juncture rests a star emanating
nerves. They are known   for *antics & prattle.*

For schottische & rope   skipping. Contralto & soprano
in harmony. *A marvel to myself am I.* Two-throated nightingale,
symmetrical rather than sideways,   they sing cheek to cheek,

but cannot walk side   by side. *A soul with two thoughts.*
Millie, the smaller, uplifted at the lumbar by Christine's stooping,
dies first. 17 hours later: a soul & a soul, orbiting emancipation.

FOR THE GREAT-AUNT
WHO ATTEMPTED SUICIDE

Slick magnolia drape over the kitchen window,
tea boiling, & the screen door locked to shut
her out. Uncle Vandell upstairs not talking

to her, playing the widower again. The kitchen
is tideless. Daughters & nieces despise him—
all barber strop & onion birthstone & clank

of knife & fork on a finished plate.
China elms windbreak the picture windows,
tv lamp on, even the nightlatch is used

against her. Uncle Vandell upstairs not talking
to her, the tea boiling away again. The neighbors
never suspect these tethered walks around the house.

Peculiar tonight her leaving the yard. The evening
sun cribs itself, night trellises its stars. She
considers driftwood & all currented things, how

the dirty river racks its thoughtless prizes.

FOR THE GREAT-AUNT WHO SPOKE IN ITALICS

—Onfirethewearygohome.

Weakness has no lilt, really. *No fainting*
spells. No housebroken eclipse. *No wild sighs*
into handkerchiefs. Their baby sprawled open
all plush & nap-fattened: his strength
comes through like teeth. *Quietly.* These rooms
are asleep, the pipes not speaking, water
rests in their elbows. *Silence.* (She pins up
her hair—fanatical crown of pentecostal
cursive—& wields her unsung tongue
over underbite: 30 crooked birds
perched in a shut place. They sing only
of things too fragile to hold in your pocket.)

WHILE THE PENTECOSTAL MEN
ARE IN THEIR CARS, *A FANTASY*

The women, in pentecostal tongue,
percolate. The baptismal
twentyfour in the river at dawn,

they

wash away the clothes
of miscarried daughters, fathom

the mud again & shores
according to water. The women

unpin

their hair & the water stops
rolling. They pin up again their hair
& the river, pinned up, goes to church.

THE GREAT-AUNT MEETS
THE COLORED NURSE

The way a knuckle of ginger heals, she.
In hospital bed 420A, drugged to sleep,
restrained, Vietnam on tv, catheter. *She*

doesn't have it so easy. A big woman twice
removed and raw, she dreams of helicopters
cutting into jungle. Bouquets crowd its floor,

overwhelming snipers with petal-stench. She
wakes, wishes she were popular. The stroke
in 420B gets no felt daisy in a milk-glass vase;

kimono in a coma she gets roses roses roses.
420B—soused daily with Estée Lauder by
a gassy daughter who doesn't watch

the right soaps—annoys the scent-sensitive
420A whose husband, my uncle, gave her 6
roses, the guilty ones, every time he bought

a dozen. (*Cheater cheater,* he died in his car
at 2 a.m. parked under the mimosa right outside
his own house, his pants down, his hat on, his

heart attacking. *Ha.*) She retreats into the cradle
of her arm, where absence nurses with teeth.
Should the Rapture insist, her body will nod

yes. Never before has her body ever said
of course. Never again will her body ever say
completely, so she thinks as a brisk little nurse

gives a sadistic spit bath. 420A complains
to that little red button at the bedside
and the nurse in charge of recovery

takes over washrag and bandage with hands
that have never touched—ever before in the life
of a shotgun's daughter.... In 420A a woman

sobs, gauze off behind a sterile curtain. This nurse
so gentle it shocks her sad. The news fires up
above them, a riot in static on the perched tv. My aunt

wants to know of the nurse her name, does she crochet,
do tassels? As she tells it she invites her to supper. The table
is never set—but the nurse receives a shawl in the mail

at Christmas with a baby Jesus card
that says *God Bless You,* signed illegibly.

FOR THE GREAT-AUNT WHO NEVER MARRIED

A lettuce leaf in soup will take up the grease.
If hiccups, drink water through a handkerchief.
Bury a rooster twice as deep as coon dogs dig.
Restring pearls once a dozen town trips, else

the floss knots get dingy. Hide his first name,
bottom of the button box. Whisper it to the well
spiders. Never ask God for a single thing. Always
dry white stockings in a dark room. Take the shine

off a black dress. Boil clothespins. Weep. Into
sinkholes. Into a nest of hull & feather. Coal fire
noiselessly in sickrooms. Hush windows with gauze.
Pray for loved ones in alphabetical order. Ugly match

scratches on white walls? Cat pee on suede slippers?
Mother clouding the vinegar? Feather ticking
stinking of a dying old woman? Try bicarbonate
of soda under the arms. Lye in frozen drainpipes.

Mahogany cake with sleeping powders. Salt the pillow.
Slip away to meet him & your mouth goes dry. Creeks
run over—it's spring—& maybe she'll nap her heart
stopped. (To the bright hand of God like a moth

she'll swing.) Hyperacidity? Dirty velour? Wall mice?
Foreign body in eye? To know if the telephone rings
while you're away: carbon paper between clapper & bell.
Open your mouth every other kiss. He'll love you

more. Or he won't love you at all. Never
be jealous of your mother just because she's dying
a widow. Don't hate men that cuss. Don't cuss men.
Restring your pearls again. Turn the mattress. Turn

her bed to face east. Turn the house inside out.

FOR THE GREAT-AUNT WHO MARRIED TWICE

It was divorce when I pawned the ring, she
answers her fiancé. Joppa to Metropolis
across the bridge from Kentucky, married
on the way & honeymooning a new year
lease on two rooms north of Southside
Motors with a diamondless needle
on the record player & nothing
else to do. *Put my hands away.*

The mattress springs in shivaree blather
me in virgin key. Behind blue-dot draperies,
Husband 2 I rise for you: be-bop of biscuit
dough. I am blind knocking in black stockings
& bigamy in brand new bikini. & you—brooder
of my brouhaha—blinkered by blankets,
you are my all time favorite.

Unbraid my hair. Last-minute & bathwater
running all out hot blares an encore steaming
of their make-do wedding clothes
(flagged across shut windows)
before going out to the restaurant
where paper roses fret over candlelight
& the piano player is colored. *Undo it slow.*

FOR THE GREAT–AUNT WHO DIALED 555

Soapstars mingle twelve steps at a time, toasting her
with sparkling cider,
paparazzi in constellation. Phoebe Wallingford

raises her bubbly and my great-aunt
offers the reporter a cheese on cheese cracker sandwich.
He refuses. I take two. She does not turn down the television.

We are not alone, she quotes her husband. *The miraculous*
all around us: duckbilled platypus, Loch Ness, abominables.

*

My grandfather's brother is 76 and lost in the Pacific Northwest
searching the boggy creeks for tracks to plaster-cast, for a myth
to videotape, for a dark man or a man in the dark or the dark itself

as it dwells in the vanishing woods

sweating through its hairy suit. My aunt has given twelve
interviews since she rang the police to tell them neither her
husband nor his Sasquatch have returned from what she titles

Ed's Safari.

Today is her fifth day as front page competition

for the Mississippi, flooding
into August. We rouge to impress *The Gazette*.

*

For the great-aunt who kidnaps any spotlight.
Who matches any camera's dime-splitting flash

with a loot of hip and dimple. Who pranks
neighbors and religious channel prayer warriors
and my mom. Who on a dare when she was 28

called *Lucy* at Klondike 5. Who dared me
to call *Barney Miller* and ask for Fish.

Who never dresses down
for *All My Children*, such carbonated galas
as the bomb-threatened dedication

of a hospital's new wing. She hushes us.
She's got to see this. Some Hungarian ex-husband
declares to Erica Kane: "This isn't how I wanted you to find out

I was still alive."

*

If the freak show wouldn't come to us
he'd take us to the freak. He always had to see it

first, show me second. We'd gawk—

hold hands. He'd ask to kiss me
in the shadow of the hermaphrodite

and others propped upright, barked about,
primate. I hope he brings me back a souvenir,

a horrible toe.

CLEOPATRA

I first saw Claudette Colbert when I was eight
years old and said my death will come
in a basket of snakes.   Everywhere, I saw asps.
In babydoll bottles, crowding
toward the nipple.   I saw them as African
beans long and sullen in my mother's soup,
darting at her when the spoon broke
the surface, biting her tongue and coiling
into a mouthful of vicious spit curls.
I saw them fastened around my father's
wrists, under the starched cuffs of the shirt
the mortician picked out, scouring
off bland makeup to expose simple
scars, fastidiously cut.

Elizabeth Taylor in 1963 lounged with Richard
Burton and I was married
to a man weak like my father, baking hams
and cobblers, crying for babies,
groping my pregnant stomach from behind
as if he was carrying.   I didn't want
the child, I didn't want my breasts
too swollen to force into the mouths
of asps, small as keyholes.   I wanted
to die before I let any part of myself
be taken, even by a weak man.   I could snap

my fingers and he would dance like Cleopatra's
chorus line of girls clad in their Egyptian
gowns of golden cutlery   and I would laugh,
lift my maternity blouse and say   *Dance,*
you idiot, dance for the kingdom
you can never know.

CONVERSATION, *A FANTASY*

You are even taller in the dark.	I am taller than the dark.
How did you find me here?	I heard spit collecting in your mouth.
There's money in my purse.	Never enough.
Take what you want.	All but the pulse.
I've never done anything to you.	I want to do something to you.
I'm not even pretty.	You never were.
And you want me anyway?	I always wanted you.
Do you hear the sirens?	I'll take them with me when I leave.

NOTES

Daring Love: I dedicate this poem to my mother. I do not claim that you are therein represented, yet I so want you to understand.

Mema's Hat: For my mother in memory of her mother in memory of her mother....

The Undescending Man: The root of the word *hermaphrodite* involves the Greek myth of the too-cool Hermaphroditus. The nymph he rejects is heard by the gods. When he swims in her spring, she swims with him: their bodies unite.

Georgette Was a Hip Queer: Based on the chapter, "The Queen Is Dead" from Hubert Selby Jr.'s novel *Last Exit to Brooklyn* (1957) and sequences in the film adaptation by Uli Edel (1990).

Buckshot: In the mid-nineties, reports circulated that Nina Simone in Aix-en-Provence, France, received an eight-month suspended sentence for firing buckshot at neighbor kids making too much noise. This poem draws on an array of poems and songs (Nikki Giovanni, Paulette C. White, Lauryn Hill) about Nina Simone, reviews of her albums and concerts (Albert Goldman in *Life*, among others), articles about her (especially Maya Angelou's "Nina Simone: High Priestess of Soul" in *Redbook*, November 1970), and interviews with her. As well: her autobiography *I Put a Spell On You* (1991). Dr. Simone's repertoire includes Brecht/Weill ("Pirate Jenny"), Gershwin's "I Loves You, Porgy" (her first hit in 1958 for Bethlehem Records), and "Obeah Woman" (from *It Is Finished!,* her last album before emigrating to Africa in the mid-seventies), and her own compositions, many of which served as Civil Rights movement anthems ("Mississippi Goddam," "Backlash Blues," and "Four Women").

No Moon, No Curtain: For Matthew Scott. *I wished too bad.*

Nurse, *a fantasy:* For Nancy K. Miller, who might understand.

The Radium Dial: Based on Carole Langer's documentary *Radium City* (1987). Dedicated to Langer, to Marie Rossiter, and to the persistent geiger-man Ken Ricci. "Gadget complete" quote from *The Day After Trinity* (John Else, 1980), about the making of the atomic bomb. Argonne, a $65,000,000 atomic research project, opened in 1948, just 70 miles from Ottowa, Illinois (home of Radium Dial/Luminous Processes factories); results were not disclosed to the thousands of former dial painters tested there.

The Pocketbook Women of You-Be-Dam Holler: For Catherine Bowman.

A Marvel To Myself Am I: In England, where slavery had been abolished, the suit over infants Millie and Christine (1851-1912) hinged not on J.P. Smith's legal ownership of them in North Carolina. Only their biological mother could legally claim them. Back in the States, Mr. Smith and his wife educated and toured with the slave twins. During the Civil War, Mr. Smith

to tour with Mrs. Smith out of loyalty. The title is from a song the twins wrote and performed. "A marvel to myself am I, / As well to all who passes by.... / I love all things that God has done, / Whether I'm created two or one." Their epitaph: "A soul with two thoughts. Two hearts that beat as one." (The poem mentions conjoined twins "Radica-Doadica"—the Indian-born Orissa sisters—who years later were tots in England like Millie and Christine, far away from home and on exhibit.)

For the Great-Aunt Who Never Married: For Miss Opal Watkins (1912-2000).

For the Great-Aunt Who Married Twice: After "Thou Swell," as performed by Betty Carter accompanied by Ray Bryant (*Meet Betty Carter and Ray Bryant*, 1955).

For the Great-Aunt Who Dialed 555: "555" is the fictional prefix for any telephone number mentioned in a television show, movie, or novel. In the time of "I Love Lucy" you would hear her asking the operator to connect her to "KL5-" or "Klondike 5."

Cleopatra: Claudette Colbert played Cleopatra in Cecil B. De Mille's legendary 1934 film. Taylor and Burton—then married—played Cleopatra and Antony in Joseph L. Mankiewicz's 1963 remake.